S0-ADU-354

CARLI LLOYD

by Elizabeth Raum

AMICUS HIGH INTEREST • AMICUS INK

Amicus High Interest and Amicus Ink are imprints of Amicus
P.O. Box 1329, Mankato, MN 56002
www.amicuspublishing.us

Library of Congress Cataloging-in-Publication Data
Names: Raum, Elizabeth, author.
Title: Carli Lloyd / by Elizabeth Raum.
Description: Mankato, Minnesota : Amicus, 2018. | Series: Pro Sports
 Biographies | Includes index. | Audience: K to Grade 3.
Identifiers: LCCN 2016057217 (print) | LCCN 2016058339 (ebook) | ISBN
 9781681511320 (library binding) | ISBN 9781681521633 (pbk.) | ISBN
 9781681512228 (ebook)
Subjects: LCSH: Lloyd, Carli, 1982---Juvenile literature. | Women soccer
 players--United States--Biography--Juvenile literature.
Classification: LCC GV942.7.L59 R38 2018 (print) | LCC GV942.7.L59 (ebook)
 | DDC 796.334092 [B] --dc23
LC record available at https://lccn.loc.gov/2016057217

Photo Credits: AP Photo/Tony Gutierrez cover; Manny Flores/Cal Sport Media/Alamy Live News 2; Trask Smith/ZUMA Wire/Alamy Live News 4-5; Matt Jacques/Alamy Live News 6-7; Brad Smith/ISI/REX/Shutterstock 8-9; Rick Rowell/Cal Sport Media/Newscom 11; Scott Bales/YCJ/Icon SMI/Newscom 12; AP Photo/Ben Curtis 14-15; AP Photo/Scott Heppell 16-17; Mike Hewit/FIFA via Getty Images 18-19; Ben Nelms/REUTERS/Alamy Stock Photo 20-21; Cal Sport Media via AP Images 22

Editor: Wendy Dieker
Designer: Aubrey Harper
Photo Researcher: Holly Young

Printed in the United States
of America

HC 10 9 8 7 6 5 4 3 2 1
PB 10 9 8 7 6 5 4 3 2 1

TABLE OF CONTENTS

SOCCER STAR

Carli Lloyd dribbles the soccer ball down the field. She kicks. Goal! The Dash win! Carli Lloyd scores when it matters most. She is a soccer star.

MIDFIELDER

Lloyd is a world soccer star. She plays for Team USA. She also plays pro soccer in the U.S. and Europe. Lloyd is a **midfielder**. She has two jobs on the field. She helps the **defenders**. She also makes goals.

WORKING HARD

Lloyd grew up in New Jersey. She was a soccer star in school. In 2002, she joined the U.S. junior national soccer team. Other players were better. Lloyd hired a coach to help. She practiced. She worked hard.

Lloyd still trains every day. She even trains on holidays.

TEAM USA

In 2005, Lloyd joined the U.S. Women's National Soccer Team. Lloyd's hard work paid off. In 2007, she was named the **MVP** of the famous Algarve Cup in Portugal.

U.S. SOCCER

In 2008, Lloyd joined a new U.S. pro team. She has played for many U.S. teams. She got her start with the Chicago Red Stars. By 2015, she was playing for the Houston Dash.

In 2017, Lloyd joined England's Manchester City team for their spring league.

GOLDEN YEAR

The year 2008 was a big one for Lloyd. Team USA won the gold medal at the Olympics. Lloyd also was named the U.S. Soccer Athlete of the Year.

WINS AROUND THE WORLD

Team USA continued to win world matches. Lloyd helped the team win 2nd place in the 2011 World Cup. They won another gold medal in the 2012 Olympics.

GOAL! GOAL! GOAL!

In the 2015 World Cup, Lloyd played one of her best matches. She made three goals in one game. That's called a **hat trick**. Team USA won the World Cup.

No other woman has gotten a hat trick in a World Cup game.

PLAYER OF THE YEAR

Lloyd has won many top soccer awards. In 2015, she won the World Cup **Golden Ball** and **Silver Boot**. **FIFA** also named her the Player of the Year in 2015 and 2016. Carli Lloyd is a superstar.

Lloyd was named "Player of the Year" in high school, too. It is a title she's used to.

JUST THE FACTS

Born: July 16, 1982

Hometown: Delran, New Jersey

College: Rutgers University

International debut: 2005

Teams: Houston Dash; U.S. Women's National Team; Manchester City, England

Position: Midfielder

Accomplishments:

- U.S. Soccer Female Athlete of the Year: 2008, 2015

- World Cup medalist: 2007 (bronze), 2011 (silver), 2015 (gold)

- Olympic Gold medalist: 2008, 2012

- FIFA World Cup Golden Ball: 2015

- FIFA World Cup Silver Boot: 2015

- FIFA World Player of the Year: 2015, 2016

WORDS TO KNOW

defender – a player who works to stop the other team from scoring

FIFA – the organization that makes rules for soccer matches around the world

Golden Ball – an award given to the best player in the World Cup

hat trick – when a single player makes three goals during one match

midfielder – a player who plays in the middle of the field; she tries to prevent the other team from scoring and brings the ball forward to score for her own team.

MVP – stands for Most Valuable Player

Silver Boot – an award given to the second-best goal scorer in the World Cup games; the best scorer wins the Golden Boot.

LEARN MORE

Read More

Fishman, Jon M. *Carli Lloyd*. Minneapolis: Lerner Publications, 2016.

Jökulsson, Illugi. *U.S. Women's Team: Soccer Champions*. New York: Abbeyville, 2015.

Websites

Carli Lloyd: The Official Website
www.carlilloyd.com/

Carli Lloyd Soccer | Team USA
www.teamusa.org/us–soccer/athletes/Carli–Lloyd

INDEX

Every effort has been made to ensure that these websites are appropriate for children. However, because of the nature of the Internet, it is impossible to guarantee that these sites will remain active indefinitely or that their contents will not be altered.